Bottle Tree

Acknowledgments

For their support and encouragement over the years, many thanks go to my family, especially Don Noble, Julie Noble, Jenny Noble-Kuchera, Mary Horne, and Dick and Nancy Horne; friends and colleagues, especially Mark Dawson, Sharon Devaney-Lovinguth, Rachel Dobson, Gretchen McCullough, and Wendy Reed; and teachers, especially Thomas Rabbitt. My mother, Josephine "Dodie" Walton Horne (1934-1994), was the first poet I knew, and my first poetry teacher; her enthusiasm for life and love of good writing sustain me to this day.

Thanks to the Seaside Institute for an Escape to Create Writing Fellowship in 1997, during which time I worked on some of these poems, and to the Alabama State Council on the Arts for a Literature Fellowship in 2008. Thanks also to the Alabama Writers' Forum and the Limestone Dust Poetry Festival for their invaluable efforts in creating literary communities, and to the Department of English at the University of Alabama, the City of Northport/Rose Fine Arts Initiative, and Kyes Stevens and the Alabama Prison Arts and Education Project, for the opportunity to learn more about poetry while teaching it.

Grateful thanks to the editors and journals who first published these poems:

"A Chill," *Poets On:*, Winter 1995.

"After the *65 and Over* Swim Class," *Birmingham Poetry Review*, Fall 1990.

"An *Ubi Sunt* for Certain Aunts," *storySouth* (online at

http://www.storysouth.com/), July 2006.
"The Attendant at the College Street Laundromat,"
Noccalula, Vol. 3, 1998.

"Beach Pieces," Limestone Dust Festival Anthology,
published by the Limestone Dust Festival, Huntsville,
Alabama, 2003.

"Black Is the Color of My True Love's
Hair,"*Amaryllis*, Vol 8, 2001.

"Chicago," *PMS: Poem Memoir Story*, Number 7, 2007.

"Chinese Women Gathering Pecans in Tuscaloosa,
Alabama" (published as "Chinese Women Gathering
Pecans Beneath Trees in Tuscaloosa, Alabama"), in
Lonzie's Fried Chicken, Summer/Fall 1999.

"Cicada Song," *Wingspan*, Jefferson State Community
College, 2008.

"Comets and Other Bodies," Limestone Dust Festival
Anthology, published by the Limestone Dust Festival,
Huntsville, Alabama, 2003.

"Concert," *Amaryllis*, 1999.

"The Day of the Big Band Is Gone," *Lonzie's Fried
Chicken*, Summer/Fall 1999.

"Detroit Diary," Limestone Dust Festival Anthology,
published by the Limestone Dust Festival, Huntsville,
Alabama, 2002.

"Early Summer, South Alabama," *Amaryllis*, Vol 8, 2001.

"Est. 1846," *Birmingham Poetry Review*, 1996.

"The Fourth Thursday in November," *Nantahela Review,* August 2009.

"Habitation," *Old Red Kimono,* May 1996.

"Last Swim," *Birmingham Arts Journal,* October 2006.

"The Mallettown Bridge," *Noccalula,* Vol. 3, 1998.

"Miss Betty's School of Dance," *Amaryllis,* 1996.

"Monday Morning with Household Chores," *Motif: Writing by Ear* (anthology), Motes Books, Louisville, Kentucky, 2008.

"Noon on Wednesday," *storySouth* (online at http://www.storysouth.com/), July 2006.

"North of Conway," *Mockingbird,* 1994.

"'The Oldest Living Survivor of the Titanic,'" *Astarte,* Fall 1992.

"Only Child," *Noccalula,* Vol. 3, 1998.

"Petit Jean," *Arkansas Literary Forum* (online at http://www.hsu.edu/alf/), Fall 2005.

"Preservation of Life," in the anthology *Working the Dirt: An Anthology of Southern Poets,* NewSouth Books, 2003.

"The Problem of a God Both Merciful and Omnipotent," *Arkansas Literary Forum* (online at http://www.hsu.edu/alf/), Fall 2005.

"She Wakes in a State of Elation," *Sycamore Review,* Winter 1991.

"The Shepherd of Five Points," *Amaryllis*, Vol 8, 2001.

"Source," *The Old Red Kimono*, Spring 1991.

"Southern Funeral," Limestone Dust Festival Anthology, published by the Limestone Dust Festival, Huntsville, Alabama, 2002.

"Summer Evening, On the Way Home," Limestone Dust Festival Anthology, published by the Limestone Dust Festival, Huntsville, Alabama, 2004. Reprinted in *Best of Austin Poetry*.

"We Imagine Our Mother Is Famous," published as "How We Imagine the Famous, as Our Mother," *Carolina Quarterly*, Winter 1990.

"With Dad at the Arkansas Travelers Game, 1969," *Fan Magazine*, Fall 1996.

"WPA," *storySouth* (online at http://www.storysouth.com/), July 2006. Reprinted in *Whatever Remembers Us: An Anthology of Alabama Poetry*, edited by Sue Brannan Walker and J. William Chambers. Mobile, AL: Negative Capability Press, 2007.

Notes

The *Encyclopedia of Southern Culture* entry on bottle trees is by Jim Martin, Yazoo City, Mississippi, pp. 495-496.

I first discovered the Eudora Welty story "Livvie" and the description of bottle trees on the web page of Sherry Austin:

http://www.sherryaustin.com/gpage.html.

for Don

"*Bottle trees are a product of southern black culture with roots in the animistic spiritualism and totemism of several African tribal cultures. Glassblowing and bottle-making existed as far back as the ninth century in Africa, and the practice of hanging found objects from trees or huts as talismans to ward off evil spirits also existed. The bottle tree was a Kong-derived tradition that conveyed deep religious symbolism.*

The bottle tree was once common throughout the rural Southeast. Trees were made by stripping the foliage from a living tree, with upward-pointing branches left intact. Bottles were then slipped over these branch ends.

. . . Folk custom dictated that spirits would enter the bottle because of the bright colors and become trapped. When the wind blew and shook the tree, the spirits would be heard moaning inside the bottles."

—from *The Encyclopedia of Southern Culture*

"*Out front was a clean dirt yard with every vestige of grass patiently uprooted and the ground scarred in deep whorls from the strike of Livvie's broom. Rose bushes with tiny blood-red roses blooming every month grew in threes on either side of the steps. On one side was a peach tree, on the other a pomegranate. Then coming around up the path from the deep cut of the Natchez Trace below was a line of bare crape-myrtle trees with every branch of them ending in a colored bottle, green or blue. There was no word that fell from Solomon's lips to say what they were for, but Livvie knew that there could be a spell put in trees, and she was familiar from the time she was born with the way bottle trees kept evil spirits from coming into the house—by luring them inside the colored bottles, where they cannot get out again. Solomon had made the bottle trees with his own hands over the nine years, in labor amounting to about a tree a year, and without a sign that he had any uneasiness in his heart, for he took as much pride in his precautions against spirits coming in the house as he took in the house, and sometimes in the sun the bottle trees looked prettier than the house did.*"

—from "Livvie," *The Wide Net,* by Eudora Welty

Table of Contents

First Bottle

Chinese Women Gathering Pecans in Tuscaloosa, Alabama

Which of these is kinder to the eye?

The figures of the three women
padded and bundled against a chill day,
leaning their heads together to confer.

The symmetry:
three old trees, three old women,
providing for each other.

Their fat sacks, bulging with nuts
to be cracked later and savored
for the dry and chewy sweetness.

Second Bottle

Habitation

Make three wishes:
one on a shooting star,
one on a white horse,
one on a cock-eyed car.

Under the dirt
in the big clay pot,

a toad lies sleeping.
He rests among rocks.

The bearded-iris bulb
sends out its first,

flat, green shoots.
Shamrocks for luck,

cactus for protection,
elephant garlic

for something
sweet and pungent

among the hard knobs
of exposed oak roots.

The dogs bark at nothing,
the lights inside flicker,

a long branch falls from a tree
near the house.

The spirit of the place
reminds us whose it is,

how temporary our plantings,
how rapid the seasons.

Cicada Song

For years I lay in the dark.
What went on above me didn't touch me.
A day came
when something said "move."
In darkness I struggled,
drawn by a deep memory.

Finally, a new world:
light, an openness that scared me.
Also the discovery there were others like me.
My hardened shell came off
without much trouble.
Now I am so new my skin gleams.

Last Swim

Longed-for, during the first, busy days of fall,
dreamt-of, through a dull hour,
my mind floating like the blue raft
adrift on the green lake—
I meant to have that last swim,
feel the springs shooting up
from the cool heart of the world,
smell the fecund lakebed once again
before it closed into mystery,
keeping its secrets in the mouths of fish.

Suddenly I realize I've missed it.
The last bright day is gone.
September 20th:
the surprise lilies are up,
and all the wild magnolias
are dropping their canoe-shaped leaves
in unison. This afternoon,
rain will settle in like a mild cold.
Gone are the cloudbursts, sudden thunder,
the blazing steam that follows.

I stow the rafts, put away my suit,
sow some lettuce seeds.
The kind eye of the sun
is turned toward me now,
not that other, unrelenting, blesséd fire.

Summer Evening: On the Way Home

Old man rocking on his small front porch.
Old man riding in the back of a truck.
Old man in overalls sitting on a curb, waiting.

Oh, they're surprised to be old. Where did their young-men
    bodies go?
Bodies that loved with abandon, that lifted stones like they
    were pillows.
Bodies that healed by morning, no matter the hurt.

My girl-body is in me, swinging a swing, climbing a tree.
My old-lady-body is in me, rising slowly from her chair to
    feed the birds.
It's only time. It's only time.

Filling the tank of my car on a rise where a barn once stood,
I stand facing the last of sunset,
rare breeze blowing on a June night.

We are all going somewhere and we don't know where.
We have all been the same place but later we forget.
Rocking is the truest motion a body knows.

Third Bottle

Beach Pieces

If I could decipher the minute hieroglyphics
written on shells and sand dollars
by creatures I've never seen,
why would I then return to the beach,
the universe being no longer a mystery?

If I were dropped on a beach alone,
in a matter of days I'd be ornamenting myself
with shells and strands of seaweed,
writing poems in the sand with a seagull feather quill,
squatting, nude, to examine a washed-up starfish.

Tiny mussels, yellow or purple
lie on the sand,
open hands, an open book
prayerful as sunrise
empty as a reed.

Each shell in its setting of sand
was once a home.
Each find is a study in After.
My shell is beautiful too
and when I don't need it anymore
you can find it, drop it in your pocket,
take it home for your ocean shelf.

Castaway

Self-exiled from my safe, soft bed,
      stealing the hour that begins with sunrise,
I stand in the littoral space
      facing water, feet touching earth,
the sand strangely warm
      where the water has just receded with the tide,
as warm as my recently slept-in sheets.
      Why do I need to sleep alone sometimes?

Unlike the woman I saw at another beach
      who stood just a moment at the water's edge
then ran into the waves fully clothed,
      I do not seek the dramatic gesture. If I curve
myself into the shape of a question mark, it is
      solitude I seek, not escape.
Here I belong. Here, *I* disappear
      into bird, shell, bone, claw, dune, grass, sky.

Where do I go from here?
      I return. You know I always do.
I long for your company, the warm kiss
      of air no longer enough. It is like this,
the going away and the coming back:
      the rhythmic pull in the belly,
the moon's mute appeal, the way
      water plays itself out, eases, recedes.

Principles of Flight

You ask what I know about it.
I gain momentum, am off
and afloat on currents.
Birds flip past on jaunty wings.

I have been practicing
the etiquette of the traveler,
the grace of the grateful guest
as she takes her leave.

Our backyard garden grows richly,
I know. Have you seen
the runway lights,
how they bud at dusk?

In the middle of goodbyes,
I still can see the blue hydrangeas,
full against the white brick porch
where flight began.

Here is the resolution
to my headstrong departure:
Leaving, I savor the thought
of return to our soft bed.

Early Summer, South Alabama

Dusk. The rabbits
move cautiously out to feed.
Our steaks pop on the grill.
My appetite expands.

When we awoke this morning,
the trees had rearranged themselves.
What could I do
to make a study of love?

Find one new leaf.
Watch it uncurl,
a child's hand opening
to reveal some small secret.

Learn its veins, watch
the shades it takes
and how it falls,
and then, don't study love:

be ready when it opens.
Things to know:
a walk on the beach
is a remedy for sadness.

The raccoons here are greedy
and steal what they like.
You have brought me south
to discover my secrets,

and I, unfolding,
mean to give them.

To Know Me

It's not so hard to know me.
I fall in love daily.
I've learned these are no
impediment to monogamy:
a voice on the phone,
square shoulders, a strong hand
choosing which bell pepper
at the farmer's market.
And the whole world
of inanimate, animate
objects: all light,
roofs, blown glass,
wooden bowls, a finally-
perfect pear, and so on,
and so on, and so on.

Fourth Bottle

Rough-hewn

Bring me your fresh sweet sweat-smell, lover,
the dusty, musky odor of our big yard dog.
Tell me you love me for my crooked smile,
and that my little round belly is a pillow
for your cares. Praise wrinkles! Thank the skin
for calluses, for scars, for all that proves
what we've been through, who we are. Love noses:
long, short, pointy, big as a mushroom, bent,
broken and healed, flat, turned-up, and hooked.
Enter my doorway smelling of garlic,
bearing a bundle of roots, and if your boots
are caked with mud, shake it loose
and tell me your story. For all the times,
I've sanded myself smooth, I'm sorry.

My Body

Plump in the middle like a good pillow,
skinny at wrists and ankles, tall and sturdy,
my body mostly does what it needs to do.

I thank it for walking, bending, reaching.
I praise it for stretching, opening, embracing.
I try to honor its warnings, its yellow flags and yield signs.

I remember it before it began to remember itself:
curled as a fetus, soft as an infant,
running with all its strength through childhood.

Only when it falters do we grant
the body's impermanence,
the last honey scraped from the sweet jar.

Now, like the car I need to last another year,
I gentle my body along, keep it strong,
and, over breakfast, ask, Shall we go on together another day?

Comets and Other Bodies

—for Charles

This man who was never a lover
but a friend of my youth—
when we were all like puppies in a litter,
taking a sunny day for life itself,

reaches out his hand
to touch my face as though it's his own.
His fingers rest lightly, briefly, on the crow's feet
beginning to trace a path across my skin.

His salt and pepper hair
looks like it's been powdered
for his role in a college production
of *The Cherry Orchard*.

At dinner, his two-year-old son
stretched a hand grubby with pizza sauce
again and again
at the two-year-old daughter of friends,

patting her cheek.
The babies talked to each other,
pounded their spoons, spilled their drinks,
laughed uproariously when musicians took the stage.

So, years pass. We are lovely, shining meteors.
We burn until we stop,
flare out bright across the sky.
Hand to face, rough skin to soft,

"Freeze the moment," he'd say.
I am trying to make some notes on all our lives.

Concert

How they use their bodies—
muscle, bone, sinew, tendon—
even at the cellular level,
effort pulses
in the thrusts, plucks, drumbeats,
in the lips' pursed control,
through their black-garbed bodies,
the very same bodies
that eat and excrete,
that fail, age, and die.
They throw themselves into making
an entirely invisible thing
that is not like painting or sculpture
because it moves and flows
over and into our bodies,
enters places we'd forgotten
and lets some light in,
which hurts at first but then
feels like swimming in very cold water,
so piercing, so good
you breathe deeply and fully,
and if the hall is half-empty
when intermission ends,
it's because we've been seized
by this remembrance of our bodies,
this knowledge we'd forgotten
and now must use—we've gone
to jump into oceans, to make love
in the nearest closet, to lick sweet drops

of ice cream from a cone.
Scheherazade has sent us
off to our own stories.
Oh, tell the one about the future.

Ars longa

And it was one of those
Carnation, Lily, Lily, Rose evenings,
possibly too good to last
but we didn't care:

the lights, the children, the quality of the air—
if we never were there again,
we'd always remember this particular past
as ours, owning it and owned by it.

Innocent garden, easy motion,
hands lifting as hands ought to lift,
voices intermingling like wind chimes,
someone's soft laughter.

Whatever happened after couldn't touch that:
the memory, summoned by any scent of rose,
our smiling, still-young faces,
each of us perfectly placed and yet unposed.

After the *65 and Over* Swim Class

Bare in the humid,
chlorine-soaked locker room
of the pool,

I practice
loving my body as it ages.
I am not yet old.

The women around me,
fresh from their morning swim,
are pictures of ruddy effort,

each stroke they made today
a little choice in time.
If they are swimming

toward death,
they will be strong
when they get there.

These women are not beautiful.
Their breasts hang down.
Their bellies and thighs

have stretched and grown thick
from giving birth.
But they are useful,

and they know it. One smiles
and peels her suit down.
I pull mine on. I think she approves

its rise over my hips.
In this room, we are all bodies,
all the same body,

and I want this—
to share the green stem
that they keep tending.

The pool water shimmers
with the strokes
they left in it.

Outlines of their curved, younger selves
cut through the lanes.
They are like dolphins,

each one smooth and lithe and buoyant,
and the one nearest me
motions me in.

Fifth Bottle

Solstice

Now it becomes December
and dreams rise from my belly.
Neither pagan nor believer
I await the solstice for its turning.

The angled light of a southern winter
casts my surviving herbs
in a melancholy glow.
The time for dancing naked beneath the stars
is so long past, I forget its music.

Hunkered under flannel and down,
I sleep the night away, moving through
years of my life like going in and out of rooms.
Dreamtime. The season for going deep.

Moving underground through roots, rocks,
bulbs, the dens of small animals,
I burrow through sand, shale, clay.
In sleep I will find it: the source of the trickling spring
somewhere on the north hill of these woods.

Tornadic

The air yellows.
Trees pause in the wind.
A heavy emptiness settles
in the center of my breastbone.

Spring is always like this—
farce verging on disaster,
one moment portentous,
the next a coreopsis blazing.

Some days are linear:
a horse plowing a field.
Others, the surly weather
folds time like batter.

You might take shelter,
limit your exposure.
So many ignore the warnings
and enter summer like migrants.

You might, as well, thunder and turn,
turn and thunder, and when
the great force comes
meet him in paint, as though for battle.

Ascending Patterns

Once again I've misplaced my lightness.
Like those floral sheets I can't find,
I saw it just a moment ago.
Always, when it goes, I fear I'm heavy forever.
In winter at the beach we stared up
until our necks ached, watching each
falling star cross the deep blue sky home.
Last night I stood in the damp grass
and watched the fireflies punctuate
the trees, remembering the stars, the years
that have since passed, now I am grown.

Make me unfinished again, make me green
and light in my limbs. Yesterday a woodpecker
landed on my shoulder and set to work!
Scrape me clean, peel off the scales.
Send me swimming in my bones
until the bones themselves are extra
and I am light as a drifting leaf,
curved in a cup-shape, skimming across
still water, then I'm lighter, just a seed,
barely touching the surface, blown like a kiss
into some other, my own, existence.

She Wakes in a State of Elation

Some days begin at the edge of falling.
She talks to herself in bright sleep.
Outside, the grass lies wet with dawn.

Maybe her life began when the diver
flung his knifed body over the cliff
and came up smiling out of the rocks.

Her mind banked in its own currents,
surveyed the drop. You could survive.
Security held out his fist,

grab this. She disobeyed.
Arching with the blue pitch
of the dive, she leaned forward.

Her toes curled into the skillful leap.
Yes. Her mind took its first certain step.
She has left the wing chair behind.
She's walking on air.

Sixth Bottle

Noon on Wednesday

I.

Three years old in '63,
I think the firemen blow the siren
to help us mark the time: mid-day,
mid-way through the week.
I'm eighteen when I learn
what it's for, a defense so civil
I haven't known its name.

The first time my mother cries,
she says, "The President's been shot."
She cries again at the funeral
on TV. The next morning,
she warms herself by the gas fire
in the living room. I look up
to see her nightgown flame.

Tennessee Ernie Ford
keeps talking to Minnie Pearl
as my mother wraps herself
in the brown braided rug.
Her nightgown is ruined,
but she's unhurt. We agree
not to tell my father.

Noon on Wednesday:
lunch in the yellow kitchen,
red and white soup can,
blue and white box of crackers.
In Arkansas, we don't expect

to be hit. No air raid drills.
All our shining silos fill with grain.

At home, we're warm.
The Cold War's chill
can't touch us. We don't worry.
Our parents make us safe.
On family trips, my sister and I
sign *Peace* from the back of the Chevy Impala,
count roadside hippies like white horses.

I am not prepared for the world
to split open, wrapped as I am
in my cocoon of unknowing.
Death is only the cat
who gulps down whole a goldfish
we carry from the dimestore
in a plastic bag of water.

II.
The body bags begin their long
procession through the nightly news.
My friend and I argue How to End the War
as we walk from school.
We wrestle in my front yard
until she gives up. Regardless,
I believe I am a pacifist.

1968: danger calls at our house.
"Daddy works for the governor,
and they've made some people mad."
A man on the phone
says he's coming to shoot *that bastard*.

Another one—the same?—
takes Polaroid shots of the house.

His leisure suggests
he has plenty of time for violence,
and though this is only Arkansas,
only a minor government post,
it's now a risky one
under our Rockefeller, cleaning up corruption
in his newly adopted state.

Nothing is funny now,
especially not our neighbor,
a jokester who sticks smoke bombs
under the hood of our car,
his laughter from across the street
a cackle, like the Maaaaad Butcher,
whose cut-rate ads give me nightmares.

One autumn afternoon, we arrive home
to find the front door standing open
like a gaping mouth, surprised.
Mom steps in first.
But that's all. It's only open.
The white house on the quiet street
holds only what we own.

Something is missing, though:
we all know what it is.
Safety has wandered out
and gotten lost, where we can't find it.
Later, as we play outside,
a helicopter flies over, low,
and we don't know whether we should hide or wave.

Four Views of a Yard, from Memory

I.
The leaf pile is half as tall
as I am. The great treat we have waited for
all this Saturday morning has arrived:
to run and leap into the rustling pile
and come up lifting the leaves with our arms,
their brief levitation a blizzard of motion.
It is so pleasing how the pile can be
solid and permeable all at once.
All over the neighborhood, fathers are raking leaves.
A pungent smoke that smells like
football games, new pencils, and Halloween
infuses the air. I believe that my body
could burst through any barrier,
even the strongest arm-locks in a game of Red Rover.

II.
A thin crust of snow
settled overnight, and we have
toasted white bread in the silver toaster
and laid the dark squares on the ground for birds.
Two sparrows, brown, black, cream, and tan,
and one early robin peck at their breakfast.
A stillness prevails.
Later, we will go outside,
our feet wrapped in bread bags held by rubber bands,
our hands mittened. I have yet
to build a snowman, though I have seen
pictures in books.
Snow is not at all what I expected.

It is better—the taste of it on the tongue,
its crunch under foot, the surprise of its bright whiteness.

III.
In the gnarled roots of the oak tree
that's too big to stretch my arms around,
jonquils bloom bright yellow
in the circular stone bed.
They seem to lean forward,
reaching out for the pale spring sun,
their blue-green stems bare, their throats open.
I am outside without a coat
for the first time this year.
The hair on my arms pricks slightly
from a fresh breeze. My skin feels new.
I am learning to catch a ball
by watching it into my hands
as though the ball itself
were becoming a part of my palms.

IV.
Yesterday we put on our one-piece suits
and splashed in the blue wading pool.
The green hose stretched from the spigot to the pool's lip,
pouring clear water from its copper mouth.
Today our suits dry on the wooden rack,
now barely damp, smelling both of sun
and of water, familiar, like a washcloth.
After last night's rain, the water
is cool and still, a calm eye reflecting the sky.
One oak leaf, and two maples like outstretched hands
float without motion. A light wash

of sediment is visible in grains at the bottom.
The inflated rolls of the pool sag slightly.
A mockingbird lands, gets its balance,
drinks with a delicate dip, and flies away.

The Problem of a God Both Merciful and Omnipotent

Whole families passed through
that red house so quickly—

later, my father moved us
to a *more stable* street.

But then, for three months,
I had a friend named Nancy.

I'd go down after supper
to play until dark.

The table was the only clear space
in their house, the only hard place

her sister Lynn could lie.
Plates cleared, the family

set Lynn on the table.
They stood at their places

to stretch her arms and legs.
The first time I saw this,

I thought it was punishment:
Lynn resisted. She seemed to writhe in pain.

No one had yet explained to me
"dystrophy" or "therapy."

No one said, "will you help?"
or commanded: "wait on the porch."

I wondered how much it hurt;
was Lynn like the starfish?

I'd learned from a library book
they could grow back damaged limbs.

Growth can make you stronger.
Pain equals only itself,

leaving a splinter
embedded in the calm of the mind.

When Nancy, who could make me cry
by taking her dolls home,

came to say goodbye,
I hid in the back closet.

I burrowed down deep
into my nest of old clothes,

said "go away" through the door
and pretended I couldn't hear.

Then I thought of how the family
used to sing over Lynn.

That was what I'd miss:
their ragged singing, those sweet hymns.

The Fourth Thursday in November

All day today, in cars careful at stoplights
and moving slowly along the town's curving roads,
white-haired old ladies dressed in bright colors

have perched in passenger seats, belted-in, precious cargo
conveyed by daughters and nieces to the day's feasts.
Looking through lightly tinted windshields,

they are remembering old dogs, favorite shoes,
a sudden, brief affair, perhaps regretted
but never forgotten. They wonder

how many holidays are to come—
or maybe I simply wonder for them,
thinking of aunts and cousins of my own.

I shirk the question, the ugly one we do not ask in polite company:
Is this the last? Name it: last laugh, last merry hug,
last look at a face that's something like my own?

Tonight, a full moon like a knowing, open eye
rose over a picked field of cotton,
white wisps on frail stalks.

Such a familial moon, hanging low in a sky
banded first with blue, then pink, then a color akin to white,
the creamy white of an opaque doorknob.

Earlier, the red light of sunset
flattened the landscape we drove into.
Catfish ponds turned blue, trees flamed.

It was after stopping for coffee that we saw moonrise,
and later, much later, that it rose high,
distant and unforgiving, more judge than confidante,

harshly watching our night ride home.
So what if the feast ends, the sun sets,
the unsayable finally speaks its own name?

I hold this moment sacred around the dazzling table:
our glasses rise in unison, pause, hold,
catch light just before they touch.

Seventh Bottle

An *Ubi Sunt* for Certain Aunts

Those enervated, hypothyroidal, smoking southern ladies
clad in crisply ironed men's shirts, slacks, canvas shoes,
never without a certain amount of frustration, life being
never as beautiful or perfect as they had been led to expect—

their wry humor, dry laugh, yet nothing but praise and charm
for the children: "Oh honey, oh sweetness, oh darlin',"
as though we were the loveliest confections, too pretty to eat—
saved for themselves the scathing insults:

"Stupid, stupid, stupid," at little mistakes—spilled sugar,
a bad marriage—teaching us young to be infinitely generous
with others. I decided to retrieve their softly dropped r's:
dinner party, otherwise, suppertime, motherhood,

their language the patois of defeat, a desuetude I rejected.
They mostly died before seventy, their permanent
	disappointments
turned inward, though nothing as showy as cancer, heart attack,
stroke. Just a gradual shrinkage, the slow flaking of paint

on an old house, its imperceptibly liquid panes.
Oh ladies, I would like to clasp you to my grown-up bosom
(a word you used freely, it used to embarrass me no end),
smooth the puzzlement from the cracked glaze of your faces,

and soothe, "Not stupid. Honey. Sweetness. Beautiful aunts, aunts of my youth." I see you, in mind's eye, sighing back at me, a chorus wreathed in smoke, languid movements of the wrist: "Oh darlin'," you begin, "Let me tell you about the time . . . "

Lost. Unsalvageable. Lovely.

Fordyce

Hot in the kitchen,
always. Her hair falls loose
in light strands
she brushes from her forehead
with the damp back of her hand.
Each summer, she puts up fruits—
figs, pears, berries.
Their sweetness lasts
a Southern winter.

Her husband sits on the porch
next to the spreading fig tree,
planning his lessons
and marking third graders' sums.
His students
might be surprised
to see his stern face soften
when he hears her humming,
as she works, her favorite hymn.

She calls and they carry
the warm jars in boxes,
hands underneath for support,
into the basement.
Who would know that the cool air,
sudden seclusion, entice them,
that they hold each other,
laugh and fall easily
onto the packed-dirt floor,

she for once not worrying
about black widow spiders?
Who would expect
her swept hair could fall so full,
that his, carefully combed,
now mussed, could be so boyish?

Rock Collecting

That day I was clearing away my things
so I could move out and be married.
I tried to throw the whole collection
down our wooded hill, but only managed
a hunk of quartz too rough to be a prize.
They were all small.
They were all too heavy to throw.
Single again, I carry them from house
to rented house in an old shoebox.

Uncle Vernon, an amateur geologist
who had weak lungs,
lay on Mamaw's couch
and coughed without relief.
He roused himself
to dig out hinged boxes
of local samples
from the state geological society:
tiny chunks stuck to the cardboard with glue.

I was small but known.
At the edges of their talk
I had a place. I dozed
through the afternoon
in the old recliner.
I listened to the football game,
their talk of local politics,
the whole room
drifted and drifted away.

I'm so full of the loss
of these people I didn't know to know
and only now miss,
but now they're still as stones.
I hold in my palm a piece of bird's eye quartz,
one apache tear, mica, fool's gold.
My few small black-and-whites
point to their absence:
a gesture, a glance, but no more.

Source

—for Josephine Katherine Thach Walton Bunn

The plate is green, color soft
as sea foam, circled
at the rim by small black cats:
eight, leaping. Josephine,
the ninth life of the cats,
swirled a black-tipped brush.
The cats appeared, each one
hers, and sleek.

On time, the daily train
whistled into town, and she,
tucking behind one ear a strand
of hair, whistled back.
I've felt that movement,
a steady, sure pull,
an oar sluicing clean
through the water.

A shell she brought from Hawaii
called me to the sea.
I walked along the thin line
stretching toward the coast.
Boxcars trundled by, sparked
by metal meeting itself.
Faded initials hinted
at sources of motion.

Visiting her,
I wore the wooden clogs,
a souvenir of Holland,
sailed them like rough boats
over her polished floors.
She didn't mind. She saw I yearned
to dance a foreign song,
and I danced:

letters carved themselves into wood,
a shell opened its mouth,
I stood by shining rails
and caught the loose sparks flying.
I was forming new words
in the language the sparks
released, and I was already
on the train, already moving.

Eighth Bottle

With Dad at the Arkansas Travelers Game, 1969

I sit in the stands,
punch my glove and wait
for the foul that will arc back
to my perfect catch,
the ball I will never surrender.
The crowd will be amazed.
A scout in town for the night
will ask me to become
the first major-league girl player.

A man with one arm
stops in front of us,
blocking the field.
He yells "peanuts . . .
popcorn . . . crackerjacks."
Stretching to see around him,
I hear the solid crack
of a homer. Ours.
The ball flies over the fence forever.

At the seventh-inning stretch,
we leave. We are winning.
"Tomorrow," says my father,
"is a school day."
As we walk from bright to dark
toward our car in the gravel lot,
I clutch my glove, still ready
for the high foul
that might sail over the edge.

My Father Calls from Arkansas on Sundays

We always get your weather
twenty-four hours later.
It travels east, across
the Mississippi, at last
spending itself on Georgia,
sometimes in larger
storms, sometimes in sun.
It's weather you've sent,
you tell me, as though
it's you who allow the changes,
as though you are still the tall god
who set me on your shoulders
to touch the moon with outstretched fingers.

Willing to play along,
I carry on
our inside joke, our shared,
tacit admittance, layered
in minor ironies,
that no one controls, hardly,
what the weather brings.
All our belongings could fly, singing,
wildly across the sky.
Four hundred miles away, I still expect,
despite the years gone by,
that you have the power
to cause the winds to settle
or make them roar.

A Toast

Here's to my father, reading a book, tucking himself away
as he did in the fantail of a ship
on its way to Korea.

Here's to my father, turning sixty this year,
smiling the diffident smile of a ten-year-old skipping school,
ever the new boy.

Here's to my father, long-legged, ambling, he's Shane, Fonda.
He shines into town. At night he sleepwalks,
dreams horizons.

Here's to my father, who's as elusive as just the right word
to say what I mean, hopping a train at midnight,
heading west.

Here's to his future: I wish him good horses,
a sunset he can ride into forever, the West he dreams
calling him home.

Ninth Bottle

We Imagine Our Mother Is Famous

She sits in front of the mirror,
putting her makeup on. Her hair is pushed back

with a tortoise-shell band, and her robe has slipped,
exposing her breast. She is forty.

Her best earrings lie on the dresser.
Her neck is pearled. Watching her

dress for parties, we observe it all:
the slight bulge of skin under her arms

where the bra is stretched, the stockings gathered
and slipped over her toes, drawn up her thighs,

a last tease of a curl into place,
and she is done. She will be perfect

when she steps, one glorious foot and then the other,
into the night that welcomes her smooth, white arms.

But she will no longer be ours. All we have
is powder and scent, the way she bends

as she leaves, and kisses our cheeks so softly
she doesn't smudge her pink lips. We watch

for the final glance she graces the hall mirror with,
then the dismissive hand. She's done all she can do.

Chicago

My mother's childhood
piano teacher
came to visit
her former pupil,
bringing good sense
and her pert presence.
"Never visit
a sickbed longer
than you can
manage standing,"
she said. "If you find
you need to sit,
it's time to leave."
Following her own advice,
she stayed ten minutes,
kissed my mother's cheek,
and said goodbye.
Leaving, she said,
"She may outlive me yet.
I'm in remission, you know.
You never can tell.
At my doctor's office,
they call it
'going to Chicago'
so it won't upset
the other patients.
As in, 'Where's Mrs. Smith?'
'Oh, she went to Chicago.'
I picked up on their code,
is how I know."
I wish I'd known her

before all this talk of Chicago.
She was the kind of
sprightly encourager
you would have
practiced arpeggios for.
You would have enjoyed
her nice powdery smell
next to you
on the highly polished
wooden piano bench.

A Chill

Someone left the heat off
in her house. The air's relentless.
Her surfaces lie cool,
without conceit.

I'm alone, shivering
in my jacket. A gray mouse
scuttles towards the door,
makes her retreat.

I check the pipes for damage.
Finding none, I wrap them.
Back upstairs, there's Scotch. I pour,
drink it neat.

Rose quartz blooms
on the rough-hewn mantel. I find
a tear-drop earring in the rug,
death's one receipt.

The single note I strike
on her piano cracks the air.
If I admit she's gone, is it survival
or defeat?

A Kind of Yahrzeit

This strong wind
hollows your chest,
blows your breastbone
into gray wood,
heart thudding dumbly against it.

Home at least is warm
but the tea burns your tongue
and if the gray sky
flattens itself
against the windows
one degree more,
you will go flat too.

At last, after the wrong novel,
it's bedtime.
"Turn your sadness over
to the cool side," she said.
"You'll sleep better."

A World of Firsts

—for Mary

Forty years later, my sister tells me
it's her first memory: snow on fields,
light, warmth, a one-year-old's impressions.
I seem to feel smooth seats, my woolly coat,
smell the comfort of my mother's scent.
I strain to see her face, bending near,
drawing us both close. "Remember,"
she is saying, "your very first train ride."

Forty years later, clearing out her house to sell,
we listen to a tape she made while driving to her mother's.
"Mary," she begins, "I had the most wonderful dream
about you—of pearls, meaning inner beauty.
I want to tell you all about it. But first . . ."—
we hear her clear her throat, the engine's hum, some static,
imagine her careening down the road in the ancient Mercedes—
"but first I've got to take the Arkadelphia exit, coming up . . .
    now."

We laugh with tears in our eyes,
our loss a first that is also an only,
divide between us rocks she collected on walks in these woods.
We will carry them away, smooth granite, jagged quartz,
in our coat pockets when we leave.

Monday Morning with Household Chores

Surprised into tears by an old song.
It's my mother, not a lover, I miss.
How she sang along happily. With abandon.
The words soothed her. Lifted her, too.
I stop in the middle of mopping the kitchen floor.
Nothing to do but sit down on the steps.
Let the tears have their way.

It's my solitude I weep for.
The never-again of it.
Changeable weather. A sweet old song.
Me aging with all these questions.
She not there to ask.

Isn't every motherless girl the same?
Still expecting her phone call.
Even after however-many years.
Mopping's regular rhythm.
Lemon oil on wooden chest.
Honor her with frangipani candles at Christmas.
Sing with abandon. Abandon. Abandon.

Tenth Bottle

Est. 1846

Rain last night,
cool and steady,
washed our headstones free of guile.
Wet dawn, first-graders stand,
mothers in tow, at the bus stop.
The stones expose our plainness
to each other, reveal our names:
Young, Stark, Fair, Hart.
The children are immune to plainness.

If the crabapple trees drip
in awkward disarray,
only the mother in curlers
who observes these things
will mark it.
One pale child
watches the sun arrive,
yellow, expansive,
his memory of the beach.

The bus pulls away
and the mothers let it go.
We scatter across the graveyard
and wait for 3 p.m.

If a body is buried today,
and it is, machinery creaking,
the ground will be solid again
before the bus chuffs heavily
into view.
The line of cars,

a string of lights,
will break apart, like nothing.
No one will linger—they have work to do.

The day puts on playclothes,
takes up its jumprope.
We want to tell the children
about centuries, and our favorite pets.
But they know so little.
We cannot tell them
what they face.
Though we are face to face
each morning, we cannot tell them.

Southern Funeral

Death's cortege slow-mo's down the street
and all our cars stop. The light turns red
then green. Red again. Two patrol cars
hold that other string of lights together
at either end, and whether we want to
or not, we stay stopped.
                              It's a windy day,
threatening rain, and the spendthrift trees
are letting go their leaves in undulant thrashings.

Fellow drivers, leap from your tin cans!
Toss your shoes off, tango down
the yellow stripes that warn us not to pass.
Fling open the shiny, onyx doors.
Pull the sad ones out. Form a wavy line
and weave a dance among the still moving trees.

Poem for October

The dead have come to sit with us today,
an unexceptional day in mid-autumn, entirely ordinary,
the kind of day they like best—
a trip to the grocery store, leaves falling in the yard,
a simple dinner prepared with some laughter.
They note our beloved, our favorite, objects:
the handblown glass bottle salvaged from a dump,
our most comfortable pair of shoes, a yellow plate,
knowing these things are temporary yet admiring them.
On days like this they miss us most—
our friends, the aunt we never called often enough
but who now has forgiven us, the too-soon-gones.
They love our flesh even if it's scarred or fat, our laughs
that crack glass, they love our arguments and our making up.
Whatever they have where they are, it is not this,
this entirely ordinary, unexceptional, mid-autumn day.

Missing

Tonight I am missing everyone dead and gone from my life.
Perhaps it is November that brings it on,
good weather for funerals.
I tell you it's as though I'm a slice of Swiss cheese,
all my holes showing—
the grandmother and grandfather holes,
the very big mom-hole,
the kind neighbors, my first trumpet teacher, and the friend who
 killed himself.
I can listen to all the trumpet concertos I want tonight,
sip sherry, put on my coziest sweater, and though I will feel
 better,
I will still be missing.
I must wait until tomorrow, when I drive to work,
to see the flaming maple tree
that tears my heart and heals it all at once.

". . . going through a difficult time"

1.
I often go away
somewhere in my mind,
somewhere far on a train,
and cold in winter.
To this end I have assembled
a trunkful of provisions:
warm clothes, hot-water bottle,
thick books for months of reading,
sleeping bag, small tent, large bottle of single malt.
This gathering together strengthens my resolve:
to clear your head, go north. Keep moving.

2.
I was thinking my grief is like
something cracked and about to break:
a dam, a limb, a beam,
a submarine porthole under
extreme pressure. What energy
is expended in keeping it back.

3.
I keep forgetting and telling the truth
instead of the pleasant social lies
for which I believe I am
so well known and admired.

Oh what
will come
of this
Oh what
will become
of me

4.
I must remember to breathe.
Breathe
like my belly is a well
and I am drawing up
pure sweet water, source of my life.

5.
"The grave's a fine and private place
But few I think do there embrace."
I'll be grave and go to my grave grave
unless I tear off my clothes,
roll around in the grass a few times
like a happy horse and canter off.

6.
I keep losing the names of familiar plants.

7.
Talk talk talk.
Talk talk talk.
Talk-talk talk-talk talk-talk talk-talk talk.
                              Talk talk.

8.
Lament: there's hardly enough time
anymore for a good cry.
If the tears keep adding up,
it will take a long weep
to let them all out.

9.
Something's stirring:
wind in the trees
and a change of seasons
may save me.

10.
Empty as a bowl.
Just now, this concavity
is a desirable state of being,
pure, clean, curved,
a pale green glaze over terra cotta.

Postcript

Even if I go away
for a while
to the serene
and rolling fields
of the backforty,
I will be returning.

Neither Marilyn nor Janis,
Sylvia nor Anne,

Zelda, Emma,
Anna, Edna—
none of the beautiful, damned
early departers,
real or imagined—
will be my guide.

I love this world,
despite
its infidelities.

Eleventh Bottle

The Attendant at the College Street Laundromat

The boys come in like sons
to have me wash their clothes.

I am careful. When they thank me,
I smile with the face I wear for work.

I roll socks, one inside the other,
into cotton fists, and watch College Street

through the glass I cleaned this morning.
Tomorrow is Sunday, my free day.

My tomatoes are out, green and firm.
Chickenwire keeps the birds away.

The old woman who lives next door
grows a yard full of flowers,

but she doesn't work.
Tomatoes are plenty when they ripen.

Warm from the sun, salted,
eaten whole, it doesn't matter

if the juice spills on your clothes
or on the floor, they are wealth.

Someone needs change.
I break a roll of quarters

against the drawer and lock it back.
Tomorrow is Sunday, my free day.

Miss Betty's School of Dance

Children, you ignore cotillion
at your peril.
Turns are not so easily learned at 40.

Your parents know, as you will,
how time is hard to keep,
how, in one brief turn

ten years slide by like water.
One moment, the high school gym
is thick with drooping streamers,

the color of crape myrtle,
and your date has sweaty palms.
Suddenly, you're perched

on the hard maple bleachers
and your own child flashes
toward the basket, and you are older.

These boxes you must endlessly repeat
for me may save you
from the ones you will draw around yourselves.

Children, so much depends
on a well-performed waltz.
It is grace I am giving you,

grace you must accept,
for your mothers, your fathers,
the children you will raise,

for our town, dusty and ill-kept as it is,
so it may rise from this flat delta plain
like a woman

who is asked to dance
and graciously rises,
fitting her palm to her partner's,
feeling his light touch settle on her back.

The Fisherman's Bride

He's gone again. I wake each day alone.
The hours drift. Out in Chesapeake Bay
his boat is slipping over the waves.
I am free to wade straight into the surf
in my cotton dress,
free to do anything,
so I sing to myself, loudly.

I am no siren. He brought me here.
I could turn to sand
and crumble into the day's tide.
Overhead, seven pelicans fly,
the days of one week,
their ungainly legs tucked for flight.

Next time he goes to Norfolk
he'll take me along.
The rough men he jokes with
will measure me for children.
I'll be like the ghost crab—
they almost won't see me.
I practice moving sideways down the beach.

I'm not pregnant yet.
I could still leave.
I could carve myself
into the world's rock face.
He'd be left behind,
silent, mending nets.
The long winter months would pass slowly.
Today, I woke early.

When I reached for him
in our bed, there was no end to my wandering.
All day, I have thought
I could slip into the water and swim to his boat
and pull myself up over the side.

Then, when I saw his face
unprepared for the sight of me,
then I would know whether to stay.

Detroit Diary

The sycamore limbs,
nude and creamy,
mock my baggy winter coat.

I would curl like a dog
into my favorite warm spot
if I could.

I'm tired of huddling
into myself,
tired of walking backward

against the wind.
Would it be a sin
to give up trying?

I could bare my limbs
and then, stripped and shivering,
plunge into water

colder than heart could stand.
It would be an ending
and not the one I'd choose

but I'd have a few moments
of running, arms outstretched,
leaping acrobatically

into the air's cold hands
and almost, almost
beating this cold carefulness

in my neighbors' eyes,
almost turning my husband's
solemn morning kiss

back into the kind he used to give
in Arkansas, where at least
we woke up to the sound of birds.

Mamma writes to say,
how's Henry,
are you pregnant yet?

I'm glad I'm not,
I write back,
who could raise babies

in a place like this?
Patience, she responds,
a new place takes time.

But she doesn't know
the way cold can chop you down
a little bit each day

until you feel barely alive.
This morning,
the milk had turned

and bugs were in the flour
when I went in the kitchen
to make biscuits for his breakfast.

I'll straighten myself up,
I will, I'll sweep the floor,
and when warm weather comes

I'll make it welcome.
It doesn't do to complain
with Henry working hard

but I pray each day for spring,
gather it in branches,
force blooms I know can't last.

Petit Jean

They'll say it was for a boy.
It was *never* about a boy,
except for *Jeanne* pretending to be *Jean*,
to go to sea. How boring

the future looked, years of
needlework and waiting,
once-a-year couplings,
all horizons known.

How the world opened like an unfurling sail
when I chopped off my hair,
slipped into my brother's clothes,
and climbed aboard.

That wind filled me
so my joy was never killed
by spoiled food, stale water,
uneasy, rocking nights.

And this new land—
I, a girl from Normandy, "Petit Jean,"
seeing what few have seen.
My mates were proud of the boy.

I was up to it all,
but now I am fevered.
I will die in this new country,
far from the village churchyard

or my priest, or even—
I think of her now—
my mother, whose harsh hands
would surely reach to soothe my hot brow.

Too late to send me home,
my secret will be discovered.
Brothers, I never meant to lie,
only to live.

On this pretty little mountain,
green-wooded, above the brown-blue river,
propped against the solid
comfort of these rocks,

I will die. I gaze up at the high clouds,
a hawk soaring, my eyes
still full of horizons, my heart
set on what I cannot see.

"The Oldest Living Survivor of the Titanic"

Magnificent disaster
has given my days their shape.
Tomorrow, blue sash angled across my bosom,
I will ride in the Veterans Day parade
of Tallahassee, Florida.
People will clap and cheer,
and why not? I did survive.
I held my doll to my chest.
I held my mother's hand.
Papa and the captain
drank their way into the sea.
If I could return,
I would not retrieve one napkin ring.
What business do I have
with lost belongings?
I wave bravely at crowds.
I speak at the city banquet.
I'm taking on no more than I can bail.

Twelfth Bottle

Note Found Written on a Paper Napkin after a Banquet at Which Pat Conroy Spoke on the Topic of Southern Literature and Race

My great uncle was the
one who ruled
Rosa Parks
must go to the
back of the bus.

Construction with Exciting Event
(after Bill Traylor)

So very many things can happen in a day:
a dog chases a cat, a cat worries a snake,
a woman with an umbrella
scolds a man with a cane,
a man stands on a platform
and drinks whiskey from a keg,
and over it all, like little gods,
some birds fly and wheel,
just fearless.

Thirteenth Bottle

WPA

Hey Walker, hey Jim, you did good,
you did what you could in the time
you had to say what had to be said.
Tell me, was that God walking barefoot down the road?
We went by so fast I hardly saw him.

Some of us here
don't know whether
to save it
or let it go.
We want
a history
and it's the only one
we've got.

Why look back? It's over.

Where do we go from here?

Sometimes I think I'll have to leave.

Old Joe Clark he had a house,
forty stories high,
and every story in that house
was filled with chicken pie.
Fare thee well, Old Joe Clark,
Fare thee well, I say.
Fare thee well, Old Joe Clark,
Better be on my way.

Oh, it's not just
the white neoclassical columns,
the black jockey hitching post in the front yard,
not the Confederate battle flag bumper sticker,
or boys in the bar singing "Sweet Home Alabama,"
or even the way the "did-you-hear-about-the-gentleman-
        of-the-colored-persuasion-who"
jokes get brought out
as soon as it's just us white folks.
            "Oh shit, I just forgot she was in the room."
            "I forgot she was black."
            "Do you think she—?"
            "No, I don't think so."
It's not the apart it's the together,
not the separate it's the connect.
It was working side by side in the field,
it's playing softball on a hot July day,
and if all our sweat isn't the same,
salt and water, just like our tears,
well I'll be a monkey's uncle.

Meat & three,
meat & three,
meat & three
at the City Cafe.

In the evenin' by the moonlight,
you could hear the darkies singin'.
In the evenin' by the moonlight,
you could hear their banjoes ringin'.
How the old folks would enjoy it,
they would sit all night and listen,

as they sang in the evenin' by the moonlight.
Ladidoodah, ladidoodah,
ladidoodee, ladidoodee, ladidoodah.

This is clear:
pure hate is easy,
pure heat, pure hate is clarifying,
even dressed up in a David Duke suit
like a hot knife through butter
wouldn't melt in his mouth.

As if poison ivy, chiggers, ticks,
water moccasins, fire ants,
rattlesnakes and a hundred degrees
at 6 a.m. in the shade weren't enough.

I love the South.
I love the South not.
And so on until the ground is littered with petals.

A dogtrot is both the cabin
and the passage down its center,
a breezeway to past and future,
the one hard, the other uncertain.
Some evenings it's a cool haven,
the loud hum of cicadas,
one lone frog piping hopefully into the night
fit accompaniment for a quiet mind.

June slid by like a dream
        of dripping trees,
        something that slips your mind
        upon waking,
        though its mood remains,

sleep-suffused, shaded,
a bit warm for comfort.

This piney woods clearing,
this green heaven
where we lay down together,
sun filtering through the leaves—
we could have been the only two people on earth,
Adam and Eve all over,
but without the sinning.
If that *was* sin,
let's do it again.

Down in the valley,
valley so low,
hang your head over,
hear the wind blow.
Hear the wind blow, dear,
hear the wind blow.
Hang your head over,
hear the wind blow.

Jim wrote:
"Pinned all along the edge of this mantel, a broad fringe
of white tissue paper which Mrs. Gudger folded many
times on itself and scissored into pierced geometrics of
lace, and of which she speaks as her last effort to make
this house pretty."

A dead pine with hollow gourds hanging
against a clouded sky
is what? A warning,
a metaphor, a minor collage,
a habit? Or what it is:

a home for martins,
an invitation to nest
from people who know something about migration.

Sometimes on Sundays at my grandmother's house
after church, still wearing our starched dresses,
our patent leather shoes,
we'd beg to drive past the crazyman's house
on the outskirts of town,
his yard and home a kaleidoscope
of hubcaps and blue bottles,
old tires painted white,
crazy-quilt paths lined with rocks.
Each time, seeing him sitting on his porch
as we drove slowly past,
I'd feel a sudden flush of shame,
his creation on display for gaping children.

On the way home:
Well, it rained all night the day I left,
the weather it was dry,
the sun so hot I froze to death,
Susannah, don't you cry.

In 1936, Bill's father
worked for the Sunshine Bakery
and had to borrow money
to pay for his son's birth.
I'd say he was worth it,
wouldn't you, Mr. Christenberry?

Nowhere have I seen them.
Like Citizens Councils and swastikas,
they are stories in a book,

pictures caught by flashbulbs,
an old bad smell, an obscene wink.
I sense them as echoes, smoke from a doused fire:
here on Highway 11 is where the sign was,
this was the restaurant they met in,
this the courthouse where Christenberry
saw the masked face.
And here in Mobile is where the young man was lynched,
and here is the judge who made them bankrupt.
Would you want to see a cross burning
in someone's front yard, if you could?
I wonder, from my peaceful room,
if I would have been brave in those wars.

Harper's: "By 1859 northern manufacture provided an
annual return of $1.9 billion, while southern agriculture
yielded only $204 million; all that remained to be discussed
was whether the political revolution evident in the
arithmetic would find expression as a treaty of peace or an
act of war."

Well, I fight
against being polemical.
Still, where else
did all that wealth
come from
but free labor?

You can drive down roads
for miles on end, interrupted only
by a deer leaping ahead of the car,
legs outstretched
as in a woodland frieze.
Here, in summer,

are seasonal cathedrals
green transepts,
tumbling buttresses
contrived of heart-shaped leaves
that die to rise again
and hide, deep-shadowed,
a secret clustered purple flower.
On a lucky day you see
a kingfisher dive into still water,
dead pines poking up like fingers,
hear the low repeated cry of a bittern.
The trees have seen it all,
have even been implicated in death,
but sunlight slants equally through their branches
on evil or beauty,
and this is some kind of consolation.

I confess I'm uneasy
in these mansion-museums,
monuments to gracious living,
the style of which—
someone is saying
this is her "idea of Heaven"
and it's true the view
over these sloping fields is *magnificent*
until the docent tells us
how it helped the master
keep an eye on his slaves.
Ah, the uses of beauty.
Here is the very telescope with which—

From the raised and crumbling porch
of Saunders Hall, it's cotton fields
stretching flat as a coverlet

and descendants of sharecroppers
in the decaying big house
who overlook them.
"I grew up in this house,"
he says. "And one day some men
from the Saunders family came
and took the headstones
out of the family graveyard.
One of 'em left his glasses
lyin' on the ground,
and me and daddy jumped in the truck
and caught up with 'em.
I remember that."
Let's have another Bloody Mary
from the cocktail tables set up in the yard
and try to ignore the woman
with her head wrapped in a bandage
as though just returned from battle.
It was she who planted the flowers by the steps.
See, the dirt's still freshly turned.

No matter how long I live here
I don't think I'll understand it all
so why keep banging my head against it?
Go to Wal-Mart
and see, there, how a bargain
breaks down barriers to integration.
E pluribus unum, y'all.

Mr. Frog went a'courtin', he did ride, umhmmm, umhmm.
Mr. Frog went a'courtin', he did ride, umhmmm, umhmm.
Mr. Frog went a'courtin', he did ride, sword and a pistol
    by his side,
Mr. Frog went a'courtin', he did ride, umhmmm.

Sometimes on the porch late at night,
everybody tired from the day's work,
talking about how it might be a good year, this time,
this time we might get ahead, for once,
she'd sit in her momma's lap,
too big for it now but allowed,
on a night like this,
and dream her way into a future
where she'd be a nurse, or maybe a teacher,
and live in a nice house with curtains,
and maybe a good stove,
and there would be a man
much like her daddy but dressed in a suit,
and he would love her.

I see the moon and the moon sees me,
the moon sees somebody I'd like to see.
God bless the moon and God bless me,
God bless somebody I'd like to see.

If everyone falls silent
at twenty minutes before or after the hour,
an angel is passing over the house.

Itchy nose: company coming.
Dropped spoon: the same.
Set an extra place.

Shiver down your spine:
Rabbit ran over your grave.
Rabbit ran over your grave.

The black man on the riverwalk
asks for spare change.

People are afraid.
They have their wallets to protect,
their sense of safety.
"Spare change? For a cup of coffee?
Hey. Hey! This ain't the wind talkin'."

So often we misunderstand:
Anne Sexton wrote she was "on tender hooks."
The woman with the magic magnets in her shoes
says, "These are in the form of insults,
but they come in all kinds."
And those three families
Jim and Walker befriended
believed their lives would be changed
because, because how could they not?
This was momentous
for someone to pay them this kind of attention.
For the better?

She'll be comin' round the mountain
when she comes.
She'll be comin' round the mountain
when she comes.
She'll be comin' round the mountain,
she'll be comin' round the mountain,
she'll be comin' round the mountain,
when she comes.

At the roadside stand:
"Hot Jumbo Boiled Peanuts—
Regular or Cajun."

And I remember
stopping beside the highway

to pick a boll of cotton
and how far we'd come
from my father's boyhood,
his skin itchy from picking peaches all day,
his overalls—the symbol of their poverty—
heavy with sweat.
What a curiosity to us:
cotton in its raw form,
ragged white puff on a brown stem,
long before it became
the Buster Brown t-shirts and shorts and socks
we picked out at the Heights Variety dime store.

A partial reading list:
All God's Dangers
Let Us Now Praise Famous Men
Absalom, Absalom!
Gone With the Wind
Jubilee
A Childhood
To Kill a Mockingbird

And if I read all the books,
then will it all make sense?

Come with me.
We'll start in the chalky loam
of the Black Belt
and follow the ocean's path
down to the gulf.
You bring the beer,
I'll bring the salt-and-vinegar chips
and we'll play hookey together
on the first day of spring.

I can feel the sand now,
gritty and cool
on the soles of my feet,
and if the water's too chilly
to immerse ourselves just yet,
we'll walk awhile,
maybe as far as Perdido Pass.

Here, in this open book of sea and sand,
I can imagine a change of heart—
in the old tradition, sudden and lasting.
This is what I, who don't pray, pray for:
something new, out of the clear blue sky.

Jennifer Horne grew up in Little Rock, Arkansas, and has lived in Alabama since 1986. She holds a BA in the Humanities from Hendrix College, and an MA in English, an MFA in Creative Writing, and an MA in Community Counseling, all from the University of Alabama. The author of a poetry chapbook, *Miss Betty's School of Dance* (bluestocking press, 1997), she is also the editor of *Working the Dirt: An Anthology of Southern Poets* (NewSouth Books, 2003) and co-editor, with Wendy Reed, of *All Out of Faith: Southern Women on Spirituality* (University of Alabama Press, 2006). She has worked as a teacher in elementary, high school, college, international, and prison classrooms, and as a journal, magazine, and book editor, and has received fellowships from the Alabama State Council on the Arts and the Seaside Institute. Married to Don Noble, a writer, editor, and literary interviewer, she lives in Cottondale, Alabama.